FOR ELIZA

MEET INTEGRITY

INTEGRITY IS HONEST

INTEGRITY IS JUST

INTEGRITY IS GOOD

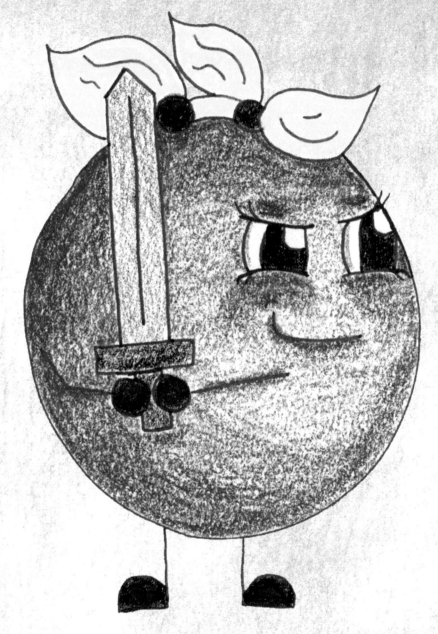

INTEGRITY IS FIERCE

INTEGRITY ALWAYS TELLS THE TRUTH EVEN IF IT MIGHT GET HER IN TROUBLE

WHEN INTEGRITY MAKES A MISTAKE SHE
TRIES HER BEST TO MAKE THINGS RIGHT

WHEN INTEGRITY SAYS SHE WILL DO SOMETHING

SHE ALWAYS DOES IT
WHEN SHE SAID SHE WOULD

INTEGRITY ALWAYS FOLLOWS THE RULES

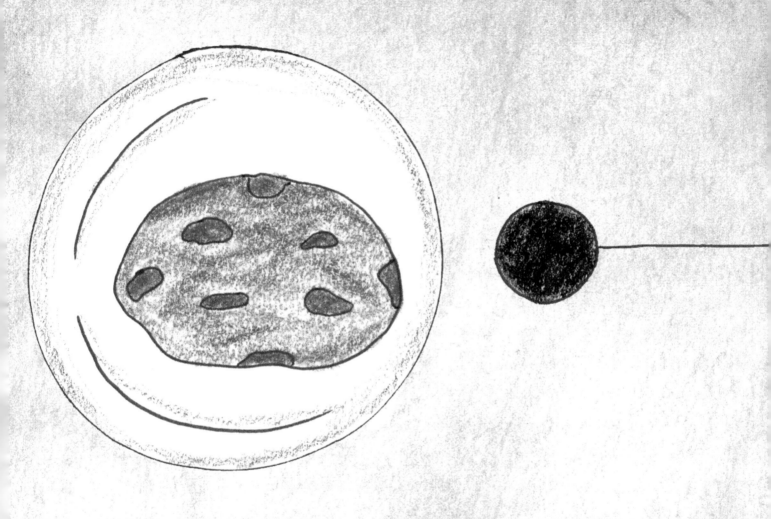

EVEN WHEN IT IS EASIER
OR MORE FUN NOT TO

INTEGRITY DOES THE RIGHT THING

EVEN WHEN SHE THINKS NO ONE IS WATCHING

WHEN INTEGRITY SEES SOMEONE IN PERIL

SHE STEPS IN TO HELP A NEW FRIEND

WHEN INTEGRITY CAN TELL SOMETHING IS AWRY

SHE ALWAYS KNOWS THE PATH
THAT WILL LEAD HER BACK HOME

INTEGRITY WILL ALWAYS SEE PEOPLE DOING THINGS SHE WOULD NOT DO HERSELF

WHEN SHE CAN SHE WILL HELP GUIDE THEM TO MAKE A GOOD CHOICE